To my daughters, Kim and Lisa
—LW

For my dedicated chess player, Ryan
—SL

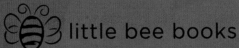 little bee books

New York, NY

Manufactured in China RRD 0423 | First Edition
1 3 5 7 9 10 8 6 4 2
Library of Congress Cataloging-in-Publication
Data is available upon request.
ISBN 978-1-4998-1306-7 | littlebeebooks.com

For information about special discounts
on bulk purchases, please contact
Little Bee Books at sales@littlebeebooks.com.

LAURIE WALLMARK

THE QUEEN OF CHESS

HOW JUDIT POLGÁR CHANGED THE GAME

ART BY STEVIE LEWIS

Judit Polgár peeked through the door of the "chess room." Her oldest sister Susan was playing, and Judit wanted to be part of the fun.

But there was more than just a game going on behind that door. Judit's parents were training their children to play genius-level chess. When Judit was just five years old, her mother taught her how to play.

Judit and her older sisters, Susan and Sofia, spent at least five or six hours a day improving their skills. Coaches gave them difficult chess puzzles to solve, and Judit memorized the patterns of pieces in thousands of games.

Judit was a natural competitor. She loved playing and rushed through meals to get back to her chessboard.

Judit especially liked playing blindfold chess with Sofia. In blindfold chess, the sisters didn't actually cover their eyes. And they didn't use a chessboard. Instead, they announced their moves aloud to each other. In her mind's eye, Judit could imagine the position of each piece and calculate its possible movements.

Judit played chess ferociously. She fearlessly attacked and didn't worry about sacrificing, or losing, her pieces. She calculated the best ways to hunt for the king and trap him.

The joy of checkmating her opponent would sometimes make her giggle—especially when playing against adults.

Judit's life was more than just chess, though.
She studied languages and advanced math.

She swam and played ping-pong.

She took joke breaks with her sisters to see who
could make the others laugh the hardest.

But at the chessboard, Judit and her sisters were making a name for themselves. By age eight, Judit had won junior tournaments and was beating strong adult players.

At nine, she was ready for a bigger challenge, so the whole family flew to the United States for the girls to compete in the New York Open.

NEW YORK

BUDAPEST

Along with other players who were new to tournaments, Judit competed in the unrated section. She looked around. There were nearly a thousand competitors. She was the second youngest.

Instead of playing in the women's bracket, which nearly all girls did, Judit and her sisters played in the open section. They wanted to challenge the toughest competition, which included boys and men. All of Judit's opponents were adults.

She won her first two games while wearing a sweater knitted by her mother. Did the sweater bring her luck? Not wanting to take any chances, she wore it throughout the tournament.

Judit's play gained attention. Reporters and grandmasters watched her from the sidelines. In one amazing game, Judit had her opponent on the defensive. She cornered his king with her rook and queen, threatening checkmate.

When he tried to block her, Judit didn't care. She let him take her rook, which left his king open to attack. Totally outmatched, he resigned.

Judit's dazzling play won her the tournament and the Brilliancy Prize, for the best, most creative, and most strategic game. She was the talk of the tournament and on the front page of *The New York Times.*

After winning the New York Open, Judit and her sisters competed as a team in the women's section of the International Chess Olympiad in Greece. Again, Judit was the star of the tournament. In one famous game, after playing a tricky tactic . . .

she beat her opponent in only seventeen moves!

In her next game, Judit was laser focused on the board. When she looked up, she saw World Chess Champion Garry Kasparov—the best player in the world—fixated on her game. Judit won and went on to post the highest score in the tournament. For the first time ever, the Hungarian women's team—Judit's team—won a gold medal.

Tournament after tournament, year after year, Judit broke records and earned titles, while rarely losing a game.

But Judit had bigger goals. She wanted to become a grandmaster—the highest title in chess—and a world champion.

When Judit was born, no woman had yet earned the title of grandmaster. Her sister, Susan, became the third. Famous world champions, like Bobby Fischer, said discouraging things about women and their chess ability. But Judit was proof that they were wrong.

GRANDMASTERS

JOSÉ CAPABLANCA

BOBBY FISCHER

SAMUEL RESHEVSKY

GARRY KASPAROV

VISWANATHAN ANAND

JUDIT POLGÁR

Judit never stopped training. She lugged over thirty pounds of reference materials to tournaments, including her own handwritten notes about opponents' previous games. Because psychology is an important part of chess, Judit studied her competition and mentally prepared herself before each game.

All her hard work paid off. In her hometown of Budapest, Judit had the chance to become the youngest grandmaster in history. Reporters pounded on her door and phoned her home at all hours. Judit didn't let the media attention overwhelm her. She concentrated on chess.

Going into the final round, she only needed a draw to break Bobby Fischer's record of fifteen years and six months. But with a win, she'd also become the national champion of Hungary.

The atmosphere in the playing hall was electric.
All eyes were on Judit.

Her opponent matched her aggressive style, and quickly their pieces were tangled in a complicated position—all attacking and defending at once. A single mistake would cost Judit the game and her chance to make history. Then, Judit thought of a shocking move.

Judit, too competitive to settle for a draw, risked it all and pressed for the win. She placed her knight directly into harm's way, setting up one of her tricky tactics. Her opponent didn't fall for her trap, but also couldn't stop her attack.

After forty-three moves and hours of intense play, Judit picked up a pawn, the weakest piece in the game. A pawn's power can easily be overlooked, but its potential is game-changing. Judit placed it down, threatening checkmate.

Just like that, she knew the game was over.
She could barely contain her smile. After a few more moves,
her opponent, realizing he had no chance of winning,
reached across the board and shook her hand.

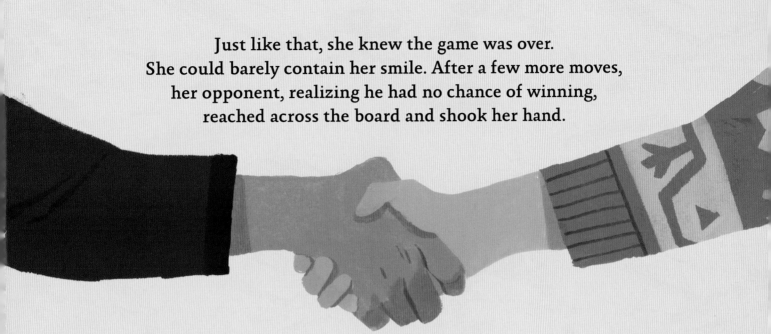

Judit won! At age fifteen years, four months, and twenty-eight days,
Judit was a national champion and the youngest grandmaster in history.

Judit Polgár is regarded as one of the most important chess players of all time. At her peak, she was the eighth highest rated player in the world. And though her record of youngest grandmaster was eventually broken, Judit's amazing accomplishments helped change the perception of women in chess. In 2021, Judit was inducted into the World Chess Hall of Fame.

Though she retired from professional play, Judit hasn't retired from chess. Believing chess connects us, she founded the Judit Polgár Chess Foundation to share her love and knowledge of the game. Judit Polgár continues to be an inspiration for women and girls everywhere.

TIMELINE

1976	Judit Polgár is born on July 23rd
1986	Wins unrated section of New York Open at age 9
1988	Becomes youngest chess international master at age 12
1988	Wins individual and team gold medals in the Olympiad as part of the Hungarian national women's team
1990	Again wins individual and team gold medals as part of the Hungarian national women's team
1991	Becomes youngest chess grandmaster at age 15 years and 4 months
2000	Marries Gusztáv Font
2004	Gives birth to son, Oliver
2006	Gives birth to daughter, Hanna
2012	Establishes Judit Polgár Chess Foundation
2014	Wins team silver in the Olympiad, playing in the open section, not the women's division
2014	Retires from competitive chess

THE MATHEMATICS OF CHESS

Everyone knows that chess is a game, but chess is also mathematics. Many of the skills and concepts used to play chess are the same as those employed by mathematicians. Here are a few examples.

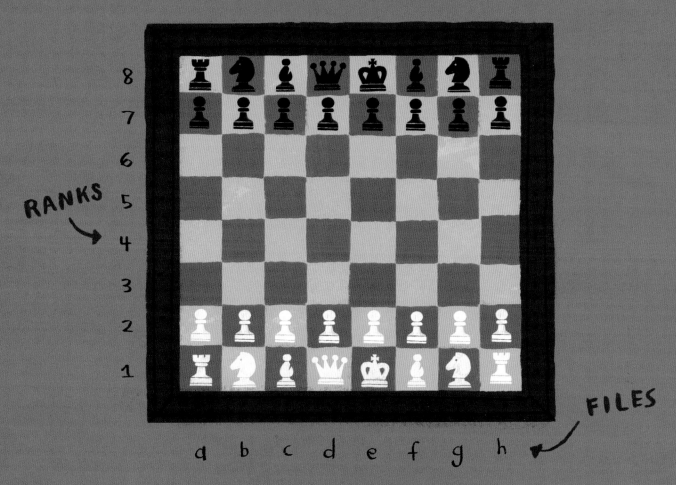

Chess uses a coordinate system, just like geometry does. In chess, this system uniquely identifies each square on the board by a letter and number. The vertical columns, called files, are lettered from a through h. The horizontal rows, called ranks, are numbered from 1 through 8.

With millions of possible moves, chess is a game of logical thinking. For every turn, players must think several moves ahead. They need to predict and anticipate the consequences of their actions. Chess players learn to quickly change their strategy, which enhances critical thinking aptitude.

Like mathematicians, good chess players have a knack for pattern recognition and spatial reasoning. This helps them picture in their minds the layout of the pieces on the board. Playing chess expands players' visual memory skills.

Being a good mathematician doesn't necessarily make someone a good chess player and vice versa. But being skilled in either helps a person develop higher order thinking skills. With adult supervision, learn to play yourself at chesskid.com!